17./5

Everything You Need To Know

WHEN YOU ARE THE
MALE SURVIVOR
OF RAPE OR SEXUAL ASSAULT

Sexual assault can be devastating no matter who is the victim.

Everything You Need To Know

WHEN YOU ARE THE MALE SURVIVOR

OF RAPE OR SEXUAL ASSAULT

John La Valle, D.C.S.W.

THE ROSEN PUBLISHING GROUP, INC.
NEW YORK

Published in 1996 by The Rosen Publishing Group, Inc.
29 East 21st Street, New York, New York 10010

First Edition

Manufactured in the United States of America.

Library of Congress Cataloging-in-Publication Data

La Valle, John J.
    Everything you need to know about being a male survivor of rape or sexual assault / John J. La Valle. — 1st ed.
      p. cm. — (The Need to know library)
    Includes bibliographical references and index.
    Summary: Discusses the phenomenon of male rape, especially of children and teenagers, with an emphasis on getting the help necessary for emotional recovery.
    ISBN 0-8239-2084-4
    1. Male rape—Juvenile literature. 2. Male rape—Prevention—Juvenile literature. [1. Rape. 2. Child sexual abuse.]
I. Title. II. Title: Being a male survivor of rape or sexual assault. III. Series.
HV6558.L3 1995
362.88'3'081—dc20   94-44981
                                         CIP
                                         AC

Contents

Introduction

*B*illy was gang-raped by three boys while in a
juvenile detention center in upstate New York. One
of the boys who raped him had himself been raped by
his own father before arriving at the institution.
Brian was like hundreds of boys in institutions
across the country who are raped and sexually
abused each year. Sometimes they are raped by staff
members, but most often by other residents: boys
their own age or older who themselves have been
victims of child sexual abuse and rape.

Shawn was seduced into letting an older man
touch his penis while playing in a park near his
home. Only 11 years old, Shawn felt ashamed and
frightened. He knew that he wasn't supposed to let
anyone touch him that way. He was afraid to tell
anyone, and he suffered from guilt and confused
feelings for many years afterward. Shawn didn't
realize that this man had done the same thing to
many of his friends who played in the park. The
man continued doing so until one of Shawn's friends
told his parents and the man was arrested.

6

Stewart began therapy when he was 30 years old because he was nervous, frightened, and depressed most of the time. He felt inadequate and unable to provide for himself even though he was a college graduate. He often hated himself. During his therapy Stewart remembered that he had been sexually fondled by his mother (she had played with his penis while they slept together) from the time he was thirteen until he was fifteen. He had blocked out these events for many years because they were too painful to deal with, so he had never talked about them to anyone. As he began to remember what had happened and to talk about it in therapy, he felt less depressed. He learned that this buried memory contributed to his low self-esteem and had caused him to hate himself for many years.

Paul was taught about sex by his older brother, Reid, who used to put his penis into Paul's mouth and into his anus. Reid threatened to kill him if he ever told anyone. This went on until Reid victimized another boy in the neighborhood. The boy told his parents, who eventually told Paul's parents. When Paul's and Reid's parents found out what Reid was doing, they began to supervise him more closely. They arranged counseling for both boys. Gradually Paul began to feel safe again and to recover from years of sexual abuse.

All of these boys were victims of child sexual

Many sexual attackers are bullies, treating others the way they were treated when they were younger.

abuse or rape. All suffered from feelings of anger, isolation, fear, shame, depression, and low self-esteem. If you have been sexually abused or raped, you may have some of these feelings, too.

It is important to remember: Sexual abuse and rape are never the victim's fault. No one ever "deserves" to be raped or sexually abused.

Many sexual attackers were raised in violent and abusive families, and they often confuse sex with violence and power. They rape other boys to avoid feeling powerless and vulnerable themselves. They are sexual bullies. They feel stronger when they make someone else suffer what had happened to them. Children learn how to treat people from the treatment they receive from those who care for them while they are growing up. Some children, especially boys, believe that they have to dominate and control others in order to survive.

The Beginnings of Abuse

According to some studies, child molestation often begins in adolescence. More than half of adult sex offenders say they committed their first crime as teenagers. Some experts believe that adolescent boys are responsible for up to 20 percent of rapes and up to 50 percent of child sexual abuse.

Boys abused by family members often blame themselves for the abuse and later in life may develop problems with anger and aggression. This may be because it is less painful to be angry than to feel like victims. Boys may begin to react to the abuse by lying, stealing, hurting others, destroying property, or getting into fights. Inside, they often begin to hate themselves and feel shame and humiliation, especially if they want to protect an abusive parent. Boys in our society are taught that they are supposed to be strong and able to take care of themselves. Often people forget that boys too are children, and all children need protection while they are growing up.

The Effects on the Victim

Some children who are sexually abused become hyperactive (unable to sit still or concentrate); others withdraw into themselves. They may try to avoid these feelings by getting into trouble, stealing, lying, or fighting. They may become nervous and irritable, unable to sleep well, and frightened by unexpected movement or sound. They may also suffer from flashbacks (involuntary memories of what happened to them) or have nightmares. Sometimes they have physical problems such as stomachaches or headaches. Often they are unable to express or experience normal feelings because they have had to block out their feelings while they were being abused.

One of the ways a sexually abused teen might deal with his feelings is by fighting.

Abuse makes people angry. But it is hard to be angry at your parents, so children often try to block out the anger. As a result, they begin to feel different and strange inside.

Stewart and Paul were victims of incest (sexual relations between family members). Boys as well as girls can become victims of incest. Family sexual abuse is especially difficult for children because it is the very people who are supposed to protect them who are causing them harm. Children are often protective of their parents and don't want to admit that a parent has done something terrible to them. So they try to forget. When they do this, they often blame themselves and end up feeling bad about themselves for many years. They also find it very hard to trust anyone again.

The Extent of the Problem

It is hard to know how many children are victims of child abuse because many cases go unreported. According to the National Committee for the Prevention of Child Abuse, at least 2,936,000 cases of child abuse were reported to Public Social Service and Child Protective Service agencies in 1992 in the U.S. Seventeen percent, or 500,000 of those were children who had been sexually abused. According to FBI statistics, there were 109,062 cases of rape in that year.

Some experts believe that these figures represent only 10 percent of actual cases. Many children, boys as well as girls, are sexually abused without anyone's ever finding out.

Many children are abused and never tell anyone.

Being physically intimate with someone can be a joyful experience when you are ready for it.

Chapter 1

Sex as an Adult

Before you read further, it is important to understand a very important thing: Sex itself is not bad. When people who are old enough to understand sex and have sex with willing people their age, it can be a very pleasurable and beautiful event. Done at the right time and in the right circumstances, sex usually makes people feel good about themselves and good about their partner. It makes them feel closer and more trusting of each other. It is a way of showing love. Under these circumstances, neither partner feels a need for secrecy or embarrassment.

This is not the case with children, simply because they are not ready for sex. As a child you first have much to learn about yourself and about the world. It is difficult to share the most private and personal parts of yourself before you understand and like yourself. Growing up is

15

growing into understanding and acceptance of yourself as who you are and who you will become. Having sex before you are ready only makes this more difficult and more perplexing.

Learning About Yourself

It is important to understand that being forced to have sex or forcing someone to have sex is wrong at any age. No one should be forced to do things with their own body that they are not ready or willing to do. Your body is the most important thing you have, and it is always up to you what you do with it and what is done to it. We all need to feel that we have control over our lives. When you were younger and adults were stronger and more powerful than you were, you had little control over what happened between you and an adult. This may still be true. But adults are not supposed to ask you to do things that are not good for you.

Of course, adults can and should tell you to do certain things whether you want to or not, such as to go to sleep, or study, or go to school. But sex is not something that anyone should make you do. Adults know that, but sometimes they get off the track mentally. This book is intended to help you realize and remember that.

Chapter 2

Tommy

Tommy was only 12 years old when his sister's husband began showing him pornographic pictures and talking to him about sexual matters. At first, Tommy was curious and excited by the special attention he was receiving from Leslie. He did not have a close relationship with his father, and like most boys he craved male attention. Leslie took advantage of Tommy's need and his curiosity to seduce him.

Soon Tommy began to feel bothered. It seemed that whenever he went to see his sister Gloria that's all Leslie wanted to do. Leslie would find a reason to be alone with him and would always talk about sex.

Tommy was beginning to feel especially uncomfortable because Leslie made it seem that all of this was supposed to be a secret. It was hard to keep secrets from Gloria, and he began thinking that maybe she could tell something was different. But

Family members often ignore signs that sexual abuse is happening.

his sister never said anything. She ignored her suspicions because she didn't want to believe that her husband would do such a terrible thing to her own brother.

Family members often ignore the signs that something sexual is going on between family members because they are embarrassed, or they are afraid to cause problems, or they don't want to disrupt the family's ways of doing things. People who ignore abuse are just as responsible for it as the abuser himself.

When Leslie began pointing out the size of the men's penises in the pictures and asking Tommy how large his penis was, Tommy was sure that

something was very wrong. Soon he realized that
Leslie wanted to do sexual things with him. That
made Tommy both excited and upset. He was just
beginning to discover his own sexual feelings. Leslie's
seductive behavior further confused Tommy at a
time when he was trying to cope with his new
feelings and to understand what to do with his
sexual urges.

Like most teenagers, Tommy was also beginning
to discover changes in his body, changes in how he
felt about his body, and curiosity about the bodies of
others. He wondered how his body compared to other
men's as well as how it compared to a woman's
body. Leslie took advantage of Tommy's confusion
and his sexual curiosity and became even more
seductive. He asked Tommy if he had ever had sex
with anyone, if he knew what a "blow job" was, what
intercourse was all about, whether he had ever seen
a grown man's penis, and what his own penis looked
like.

One day when they were playing ball, Leslie
offered him a bet: The first one to drop the ball had
to give the other person a "blow job." It was hard for
Tommy to say no when someone asked him to do
something, especially someone who meant so much
to him, so he agreed to the bet. He was afraid he
would disappoint Leslie if he refused, and that he
would lose all Leslie's attention. Of course, Tommy
was the first to drop the ball, and that was when it
happened for the first time with Leslie. Tommy had

A sexual abuser sometimes takes advantage of anyone he has access to.

no idea what he was supposed to do, so his brother-in-law showed him.

All the time that Leslie had been seducing Tommy with pictures, jokes, and stories, he was setting up this moment when he would be able to take advantage of the boy. Not that Tommy was special, but because Leslie was attracted to young boys and Tommy was the most available. Because of the family tie, no one questioned how much time they spent together. Leslie was sure he could get away with doing this to Tommy without anyone's finding out. He especially counted on the fact that Tommy would never want his sister to know what had happened.

Tommy was frightened but did what Leslie told him. After that, Leslie showed Tommy how to do more and more sexual things. Often they were things that Tommy didn't really want to do, but he became more and more afraid to disappoint his brother-in-law.

At the same time, Tommy began to feel very guilty. It was clear that all of this had to be kept secret from his sister as well as the rest of his family. This made Tommy feel bad about himself, feel that there was something very wrong with him. It was hard for Tommy to walk into his sister's house only a few minutes after he and his sister's husband had had sex. Tommy became more and more secretive, the more it seemed he had to hide. This continued until he was almost 17, old enough not to need his brother-in-law's attention any longer.

Tommy is much older now, but he is still bothered about what happened between him and his brother-in-law. As an adult, he has trouble trusting people, and he feels guilty at times even when he hasn't done anything wrong. He thinks frequently about confronting Leslie and asking him why he took advantage of a child. He hopes someday to have the courage to tell his brother-in-law that what he did was wrong.

Now that Tommy has been in therapy for many years, he realizes that he was a young adolescent at the time and didn't know how to cope with what

was happening to him. But even though he has
learned that as the adult Leslie was responsible,
Tommy still blames himself at times. It helps when
he looks at 12-year-olds and realizes how young
they are. He says, "I can't imagine wanting to have
sex with someone as young as I was then, and that
is when I realize how wrong my brother-in-law
was."

Tommy also realizes that because of what Leslie
did to him he has grown up suspecting all men of
being sexually interested in him. He has confused
attention and affection with sexual attraction; even
when other men only want to be his friend, he
sometimes thinks that they are trying to seduce
him. Tommy is learning now, with the help of
therapy, to develop friendships with other men. He
is learning that people are interested in him
because he is an intelligent, talented, and friendly
person whom others simply want to know as a
friend. He is learning to trust his other qualities
and to think of himself as good and worthwhile.

Chapter 3

Forms of Sexual Abuse

Sexual abuse and rape happen in many different ways. Sometimes it is a matter of forced sex, as in the case of rape. Other times it involves an older person's taking advantage of a child's curiosity and insecurity. Most children are curious about sex and therefore agree to do things that they don't understand or are not ready to handle emotionally. Any time an adult has sexual relations with a child, it is abuse. The adult is abusing the trust that children have for adults, the trust they have been taught to have because adults are supposed to protect and care for children. It is abuse because a child does not expect to be harmed by an adult, yet when an adult uses a child for sexual purposes he causes the child great confusion and harm. He makes it difficult for the child to trust anyone, to depend on anyone. The child usually grows up feeling confused for much

Pornography is believed by many people to be harmful.
Child pornography is illegal.

of his life, especially when he is old enough for adult sex.

Pornography

Another form of sexual abuse is taking pictures or making movies of naked children. Such films may show children having sex with other children or with adults. The films are sold to adults, called pedophiles, who use children for their sexual pleasure. These people feel safer being with children or fantasizing sex with children. Their motive is believed to be the ability to have complete control over the child. Sometimes they are married and lead apparently normal lives.

Listen to your instincts. If something does not feel right, sexually or otherwise, leave the scene.

Sexual Behavior

Still other forms of sexual abuse are being touched sexually or exposed to sexual behaviors by adults. For example, if you are shown an adult's private parts, or if an adult asks to look at or touch your private parts such as your penis or buttocks, it is considered sexual abuse.

You can usually tell when something is not right by the way it makes you feel. If grown-ups ask you to do something, or they do something to you, that makes you uncomfortable or that you are supposed to keep secret, there is probably something wrong. In such a case you should say no, get away as fast as possible, tell your parents or another adult what has happened, and keep

25

telling people until you find someone who believes you and will help you.

One of the reasons these actions are considered abuse is the way they cause a person to feel. You should never be made to feel uncomfortable or embarrassed by what others do to you. Being bothered in these ways makes it difficult for you to have the concentration and the good feelings about yourself necessary for you to grow and develop in a healthy way. These same feelings can make it hard for you to feel safe and to learn how to behave with other people.

Feeling good about yourself is one of the most important, and sometimes one of the most difficult, things you have to learn when you are growing up. Being exposed to sex before you are ready to deal with it, or in a way that makes you uncomfortable can be frightening and disturbing during a time in your life when you have so much to learn and understand. That is why it is against the law to sell pornographic magazines to people under the age of 18. There is plenty of time to learn about, appreciate, and enjoy sex when you are ready to do so.

A Serious Problem

Child abuse is one of the most serious problems we face as a society. It has taken us a long time to get laws on the books to protect our children. The first case of child abuse was brought to court under the laws that prohibit cruelty to animals. We had laws to protect animals before we had laws to protect children.

One reason for that is that for a long time children were considered the property of their parents, without particular rights. We now realize that children need protection, sometimes even from their own parents or siblings, and that they have a right to feel safe from harm and to grow up without suffering neglect or abuse.

Another reason was that many adults did not want to believe that such terrible things could happen to children. They pretended that abuse was not happening, and certainly they never talked about it.

Some people mistakenly think that if you don't talk about something, it's not happening. They think that if you ignore a problem, it will go away. Unfortunately, that is not true. Not until people are ready to admit a problem and talk about it with other people can it be improved or corrected. That is why it is so important to talk about problems, so that you can begin to solve them.

We know now that sexual abuse and rape can happen to anyone. No one is immune. Infants, children, adolescents, and senior citizens are all vulnerable to sexual abuse and rape. Boys as well as girls are vulnerable.

Sexual abuse of children has been a problem throughout history in almost all societies. Children

have always been vulnerable to adults who are
bigger and more powerful. Sometimes the adults
have had problems of their own that caused them
to take advantage of children. They themselves
may have been abused. People tend to do to
others what has been done to them: It is an
unconscious way of trying to recover from trauma.
In this way generations of abuse repeat, unless
those who have been hurt get help.

Fear of Telling

This has been most often true of sexual abuse,
probably because it is the type of abuse that is
most often kept secret and is the hardest to
prove.

Not talking about any kind of trauma makes it
worse. One of the few ways we have of recovering
from a terrible trauma is to talk about it. We need
to talk about it over and over again, to as many
people as are willing to listen and understand
what we have gone through. Sharing what has
happened to you, especially with someone who
can understand what it has meant for you, is one
of the best ways of learning to understand
yourself.

If you are a victim of sexual abuse, you may be
afraid to tell anyone about it. You may have been
threatened that if you tell anyone you will be hurt.
You may blame yourself, thinking that it happened

It is often difficult for children to tell their parents that they have been sexually abused.

to you because there is something wrong with you. Someone may have even told you that you asked for it, but that is wrong. Sexual abuse is never the fault of the victim.

Often the abuser is well aware that you are not old enough or secure enough to realize that fact, and he may take advantage of it. Knowing that there are laws against what he has done and people who are ready to help you, he counts on your ignorance.

If you are under 17 years of age and have been exposed to physical violence, the threat of violence, or sexual encounters that have made you uncomfortable, especially with adults, you may be one of the many victims of child abuse.

Facts About Child Sexual Abuse

Neither legal nor mental health professionals have agreed on a definition of sexual abuse. Certain kinds of behavior—for example, showing pornographic photographs, genital fondling, and sexual intercourse—are clearly abusive. One common definition of sexual abuse is sexual contact with a person under a certain age, usually 13 or 14, by someone at least five years older.

About 25 percent of physically and sexually abused children are under five years old; about 60 percent are between five and 14; and 15 percent are over 14. In 1989, 1,200 children are known to have died from abuse in the U.S.

Most surveys suggest that 20 to 30 percent of adult women and 10 percent of adult men have had some sexual contact with a considerably older person during childhood or early adolescence. Only half of convicted child molesters claim to be interested in girls alone. In one study, 560 offenders admitted to eight times more sexual acts with boys than with girls. The statements of school children suggest that at least half of sexual advances are made to boys. Boys are apparently more likely to be approached by strangers, more likely to be abused by more than one person, and more likely to become involved in child sex rings. Girls are more commonly victims of incest.

More than 90 percent of child molesters are men, and they are usually divided into two groups.

Boys are more likely to be approached by a stranger.

Pedophiles, who perform sexual acts with children unrelated to them, have had an abnormal pattern of sexual arousal and fantasy since adolescence. As a group, pedophiles approach boys at least as often as girls. The second group, fathers, stepfathers, and other family members, make sexual advances mainly to girls, often under stress and the influence of alcohol or other drugs.

Sometimes boys try to take advantage of others their own age.

Chapter 4

Brian

*L*ike Tommy in Chapter 2, Brian is a survivor
of sexual abuse. But unlike Tommy, Brian was
abused by a boy not much older than himself.

Brian is 14, blond, thin, and looks younger than
he is. He hasn't developed many muscles yet and is
often teased by the other kids. They make fun of
him because he hasn't grown much hair and because
he is shy and often stays to himself.

Because Brian is lonely most of the time, he was
excited when an older kid began to pay attention to
him. He thought that he had finally made a friend.
One day his new friend, Joe, invited Brian to his
house to play video games and eat pizza. Joe was 16
and had a reputation for being tough. None of the
other kids would mess with him, and most of them
were afraid of him. Brian didn't understand why Joe
wanted to be friends with him, but he was so
flattered that he never questioned the invitation.

When they got to Joe's house, his parents weren't home. Brian felt uneasy, but he ignored the feeling. Joe asked Brian if he wanted a beer. When Brian refused, Joe pressured him, saying that if he wanted to be a friend of Joe's he had to learn how to drink. So Brian went along. Then Joe put on a video of two people having sex. Brian thought that was great—until Joe took off his pants and began to masturbate. Joe said he was uncomfortable being the only one naked and told Brian to take off his pants also.

Frightened, Brian said he was leaving. Joe said no, and despite all Brian's protests, he locked the door. Brian tried to get to the door, but Joe pushed him down. He then forced Brian to take off his pants and said he was going to make a girl out of him.

Brian froze. He was so afraid that he did whatever Joe told him to do. Joe told him to lie on his stomach and then he put his penis into Brian's rectum. Brian was so terrified that he began to stare into space and pretend that nothing was happening. It was as if he were watching instead of feeling what was happening to him. He didn't cry or scream or even move. He just lay there without thinking. When it was over, Joe said that if Brian ever said a word he would kill him. Brian believed him.

Brian was determined to forget that this had ever happened, and he was sure that no one would ever find out. Matters went according to plan until about three days later when Brian noticed a stinging in his penis when he urinated. Now he was more frightened than ever. What he didn't know was that Joe was having sex with other people, from one of whom he had caught gonorrhea. He had given it to Brian.

Gonorrhea is one of several sexually transmitted diseases. It is an infection contained within the body fluids, such as saliva, semen, or vaginal secretions. Other such diseases are syphilis and AIDS. Like AIDS, gonorrhea is transmitted by contact with infected sexual fluids or blood. Sometimes, as in Brian's case, the person infected with gonorrhea feels a burning within a few days of the contact. Other times the disease has no signs or symptoms.

Brian was afraid to tell his parents, but fortunately, he did go to the school nurse.

When the nurse heard Brian's symptoms, she immediately suspected gonorrhea, and she asked if he had had sexual contact with anyone recently. By this time Brian was so frightened that he couldn't keep the secret any longer, and he told the nurse what had happened.

The school social worker was contacted, and he and the nurse discussed with Brian that he must tell his parents so that he could get help. They explained to Brian that he had been raped, and that it was not his fault. Brian was more bewildered than ever, since he thought that only girls could be raped.

The social worker told him that anyone could be

The school nurse or guidance counselor are two people
you might turn to with questions or concerns, especially if
you have been raped or sexually assaulted.

the victim of rape; it could be girls, boys, little children, or even much older people. He explained that rape was a crime. It was not sex, but a physical assault, like being punched in the face or beaten up. He said to Brian, "You wouldn't blame someone who was beaten up, would you? I don't think your parents will blame you for this."

Brian said that it must be his fault because he had not fought back, and that this disease was his punishment. The nurse and social worker explained that often victims of rape or any kind of sexual abuse are too frightened to fight. Their minds go into a kind of shock, unable to move or even think what to do. Brian might have been raped even if he had fought back. They assured Brian that he had nothing to be ashamed of, that the person who needed to feel shame was Joe.

With Brian's permission, the social worker called Brian's parents and asked them to come to school. With his help, Brian told his parents the story. Brian's parents understood immediately. They told him that they were not mad and they did not blame him. They assured him that they would take care of Joe and make sure that Brian would be safe.

The family then went to a doctor, who gave Brian an antibiotic for the infection. He scheduled another test in a week to make sure that the gonorrhea was cured. At the same time he tested Brian for other possible diseases such as syphilis and mentioned having Brian get an HIV *test. Although Brian and*

*his parents did not want to think about the possibil-
ity that he had contracted HIV (the virus that can
cause AIDS), they knew that they had to face it. They
spent several weeks in counseling before the test,
discussing what it meant. Finally they were pre-
pared—and again Brian was lucky. The test came
back negative. The doctors scheduled Brian for HIV
testing six months and a year later just to be sure. It
can take that long after infection for the antibodies
to HIV to show in the blood. With the help of continued counseling and the support of his family, Brian
began to recover from the trauma.*

*Joe's family were notified about what he had done.
The two families met, and because Joe's parents
were determined to get counseling for him, Brian's
family decided not to press charges.*

*As is often the case with abusers, Joe's parents
discovered that Joe had been sexually molested by an
uncle who used to baby-sit for him when he was
younger.*

*Because of Brian's courage in reporting the abuse,
both Brian and Joe got the help they needed. Joe
never tried to get back at Brian as he had threatened. Deep down inside, Joe did not feel very good
about what he was doing and wanted someone to
stop him. A part of Joe was relieved that someone
finally discovered what he was doing. He had known
that he needed help but had been too frightened ever
to ask for it.*

Chapter 5

What Is Rape?

Rape is usually defined as the act of forced vaginal intercourse (when a man puts his penis into a woman's vagina). In the United States, rape was formerly considered an act that was committed only against females and only outside of marriage.

In recent years, however, some states have broadened the legal definition to include other sexual acts. Contact between the penis and the mouth or anus or other forms of contact involving sexual organs can also be considered rape.

In recent years, some states have begun to include spouses and males as possible victims of rape. We now know that anyone is a victim of sexual abuse who is forced to have sex or asked to have sex but is not capable of understanding the act—either because of being too young or because of being specially vulnerable such as mentally retarded.

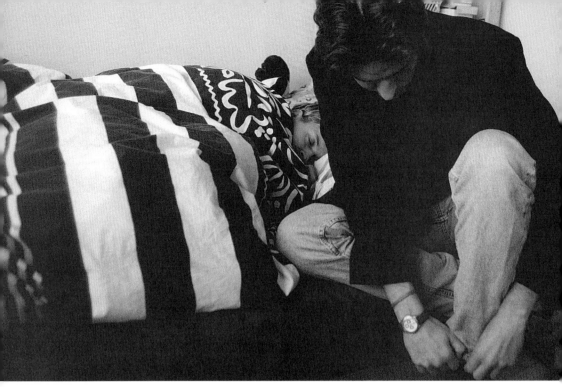

Rape is also defined as being taken advantage of when you are asleep.

A wife has a right to say no to her husband if she does not want to have sex. Children also have the right to say no to things that make them uncomfortable, although this may be very difficult for them to do. Children are taught to obey and to respect adults. Because they often do not realize what is happening or are afraid to say no, especially to adults, children are protected by law.

Legal Definitions of Rape

Legally, rape is of two kinds: forcible rape and statutory rape. Both are felonies (serious crimes) in the United States. Forcible rape is sexual intercourse with a nonconsenting victim through the use or threat of force. No actual force need be involved. If the victim—even an adult—is afraid of harm, that is considered "threat of force."

Statutory rape is sexual intercourse with a person under a specified age. The age varies from state to state and country to country, but it ranges from 12 to 18 years. Sexual intercourse with a person who is mentally deficient or unconscious and therefore incapable of giving consent is also sometimes considered statutory rape. Consent means that you freely agree and are capable of understanding the act.

What Causes Male Rape?

Rape is an act of violence. Victims are not selected because they ask for it nor because they are sexually attractive, but because they are vulnerable. For this reason, children and senior citizens are often victims of rape.

Nor should it be assumed that men are raped because they are homosexual or the rapist is homosexual. In fact, men who rape other men are more often than not heterosexual.

Studies of male rapists have found that they are motivated by several factors: (1) The assault causes the rapist to feel powerful and in control of another human being. (2) The rapist may be angry at his victim and rape in revenge. (3) Some rapists find excitement and gratification in degrading their victim; for some men, any form of violence or aggression is exciting. (4) Sometimes a rapist is afraid of his own homosexual desires, and raping another man is a way of punishing him for what is actually in the rapist's own mind. In other words, the rapist blames the victim for his own feelings. (5) Some offenders participate in gang-rape to maintain their status in the group.

Some offenders pay little attention to whom they rape. It doesn't matter who the victim is, or even of what sex. Some people are raped simply because they are at the wrong place at the wrong time— when a sick person is there waiting for anyone to come along.

Men who rape usually have very little self-esteem. They feel strong only when they can make other people feel weak. They need to make other people suffer. They rape because they are out of control and need to feel complete control over another human being.

What Does It Take to Be a Man?

In our society men are often made to feel that they have to be aggressive, and even violent. Boys are told what they are supposed to think, feel, and do to be a man. For example, I am sure that at some time in your life you have been told that boys should be interested in sports,

There is no one particular thing that makes a boy a man.

Rape is not an act of sex. Like hitting, rape is an act of violence.

be rough, fight. Whoever told you that was wrong.

Only one thing is necessary to be a boy, and that is to have a penis. If you have a penis, you are a boy. However, there are many different kinds of boys. Boys can be tall or small, thin or heavy; they can like baseball or ballet dancing. Many boys like to read; others like to build things. Sometimes boys are sensitive and enjoy talking with others. Other times they enjoy being active. There are countless types of boys, just as there are countless types of girls. Men or boys who rape often fail to understand this and are afraid that they have to act a certain way to be a man.

Does Rape Make You Homosexual?

Being raped doesn't change anyone into a homosexual: No one can be made homosexual by what others force them to do.

Most psychologists believe it likely that people are born with a sexual preference. Those who disagree often say that by about six or seven years of age most boys develop a preference for one sex or the other. But no one believes that being raped can change someone's sexual orientation.

Chapter 6

Troy

"*My father avoids me since the attack,*"
Troy told his therapist.

*A year before, Troy had been raped in the laundry
room of his apartment complex by a stranger who
had been waiting for a victim. Troy thought that if
he had not happened to go to the basement that day
it would not have happened. Sometimes he even felt
that his father blamed him.*

*Troy's therapist explained that there was no way
Troy or anyone could have foreseen what happened
that afternoon; the attack was not his fault. The
therapist also said that some parents have a hard
time accepting that something terrible can happen to
their child. They feel that they should always be able
to protect their child, even though that is impossible.*

*The therapist knew from a session that he had
had with Troy's father that the father felt guilty for*

what had happened to his son, even though it was

Counselors or therapists can help you work through the many emotions you may have after having been sexually assaulted or raped.

not the fault of either one. The only person at fault was the rapist.

Troy's father was avoiding Troy because he wanted to forget the rape. Whenever he was near Troy, he thought about it. He worried that perhaps he should have taught Troy how to defend himself better, or should have warned him against such things.

The therapist had tried to explain that Troy was frightened, and the rapist had threatened to kill him if he fought back or even made a sound. There was no "right" way to deal with the situation. Troy dealt with it in the way he thought best.

47

The therapist had also tried to explain that neither Troy nor his father were to blame for the rape, and that they both needed to deal with their feelings of guilt and shame. Troy's father had difficulty accepting these facts. The therapist knew that it might take time before Troy and his father could accept and deal with what had happened, but that it was important that they continue to talk about it as long as necessary.

When one person in a family is raped, it is likely to affect the whole family. Troy's therapist therefore recommended that they have both family sessions and sessions with Troy alone. The family agreed. It was a great relief to Troy to feel that his therapist understood what he was going through and had the patience to reinforce concepts. It took Troy a long time to become convinced that the rape was not his fault and that he had not let down his father or anyone else. At the same time, Troy's father was afraid that he had somehow let Troy down. The truth was that no one had let anyone down. Something terrible had happened to Troy, and they would both have to come to terms with it and begin the healing process.

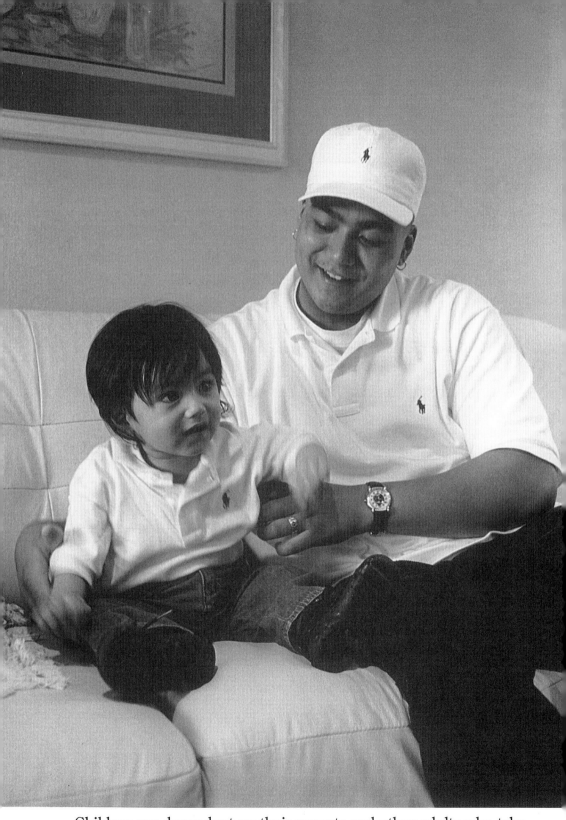

Children are dependent on their parents and other adults who take care of them.

Chapter 7

It Is Never Your Fault

Although children often blame themselves when they are abused, *it is never their fault*. In fact, the law recognizes that children are vulnerable to the acts and the suggestions of adults. Even if a child does things that he was told by an adult to do, the child is not responsible under the law. The adult is responsible.

Children are dependent on their parents and other adults who take care of them. For example, a child who lives in an abusive family has little choice about where he or she lives.

The Need for Acceptance

In addition, children need to feel that they belong. Usually they learn what it takes to belong to their particular family. They learn the family's expectations and rules and try to meet them because they want to be accepted by the most

In healthy families children learn the skills they need to become responsible adults, such as cooperation.

important people in their lives: their parents, grandparents, aunts, uncles, and siblings.

This need to belong and be accepted can help you to learn to get along in the world. For example, you work hard in school and get good grades to please your parents. You learn manners, what is right and wrong, how to dress, and many other things in order to be accepted by the people in your life.

Unfortunately, these same needs make it difficult for you to say no to your family when they ask you to do things that are not good for you. Children who are sexually abused by their families have trouble telling anyone, or stopping the abuse, *51* because they also fear being rejected. That is why counselors try to help the whole family understand what is happening.

As you may already have realized, a child's life is not always predictable or safe. Not all parents or families do a good job rearing a child. Abuse within the family is so damaging to a child because the betrayers are the very people on whom the child depends for protection and safety. The child must look elsewhere for these things.

Chapter 8

Ways to Stay Safe

There are some things you can do to reduce the likelihood of being raped or suffering sexual abuse. No one is guaranteed to be safe, but the following suggestions will increase your chances:

- Carry yourself in a confident manner, head up, shoulders back, and scan your environment as you walk. Rapists usually target people who look tired, distracted, or unself-confident.
- Trust your "sixth sense," your intuition. If you feel uncomfortable in a situation, if you feel strange or unsafe for any reason, *get out of that situation as fast as possible.*
- Avoid going to secluded places.
- Let others know where you are going and how long you expect to be gone. If you don't get back at that time, someone—preferably an adult—can go and look for you.
- If a strange man approaches, be on your guard.

Make sure that you are aware of the environment around you when you are walking by yourself.

If he seems even a bit odd or if he talks about sex, any kind of sex, go as fast as you can to a safe place—home, a store, a friend's house.

- Being alone anywhere increases your risk. Travel with a friend. If that is not possible, have a plan of action. Your plan might be to stay in sight of other people at all times, to avoid going to isolated places, and to avoid going out after dark.

- When outdoors at night, be aware that darkness increases your chances of being attacked. When possible, walk where there is the most light.

- Stay alert at all times, observing your surroundings. Avoid alcohol or drugs or anything that might cause you to be less alert.

- Never go home with anyone you don't know. Never follow anyone you don't know anywhere.

- If any adult or teen talks about sexual matters to you or touches you in a way that makes you feel uncomfortable, avoid the person and tell an adult about it, even if you are not sure what is going on. Even if the person is a relative, tell someone. Don't wait for something to happen.

- Know where you are going and how to get there. Try not to look lost or in doubt. If you need directions, ask a police officer, bus driver, or employee in a store.

- Use your voice. If someone is making you uncomfortable, say so. If they don't back away, don't be afraid to yell at them. Shout, "Back off!

Leave me alone!" Molesters often count on their
victims to be passive.

- If someone is making you feel uncomfortable
  don't be afraid to make a scene. Yell as loudly as
  you can. You have nothing to be ashamed of;
  the abuser does.
- Consider taking a self-defense or a martial arts
  class.
- Some people believe that you should not fight
  back if you are in a physically threatening situation such as rape. New studies indicate, however, that fighting back does not increase your
  chances of being hurt in a rape situation and, in
  fact, may decrease those chances. In the article
  "The Effects of Resistance Strategies on Rape"
  (*American Journal of Public Health*, November
  1993) it was reported that self-defense strategies
  including verbal resistance (such as shouting
  at someone), physical resistance (fighting an
  attacker), and leaving the site of the attack
  before rape occurs are all associated with rape
  avoidance. Only you can decide whether to fight
  back in any given situation.

Remember, being raped or sexually abused is a
risk everyone faces, regardless of their age, sex,
appearance, or sexual orientation.

If you have been raped or sexually assaulted,
you can recover. If you are not certain whom to
turn to, the information on pp. 59–60 will help you.

Glossary—*Explaining New Words*

assault, sexual Criminal activity that includes sexual intercourse, touching of genitals, oral sex, or touching of the body in an overtly sexual way without permission.

AIDS **(acquired immunodeficiency syndrome)** Fatal disease believed to come from contact with HIV.

anal sex Intercourse in which the penis of a man penetrates the anus of a man or a woman.

blow job Slang term for fellatio (contact between the mouth and the penis).

effeminate Having feminine characteristics. Young boys may appear effeminate before they develop the secondary sexual characteristics of a man such as muscles and hair on the chest.

gang rape Rape involving more than one rapist.

genital fondling The sexual touching of sexual organs, usually the penis, buttocks, or breasts.

heterosexual Having sexual interest in persons of the opposite sex.

HIV **(human immunodeficiency virus)** Virus that can be caught from the body fluids of an

57

infected person—blood, semen, vaginal secretions. It is believed to cause AIDS.

homosexual   Having sexual interest in persons of the same sex.

incest   Sex between family members.

male rape   The forcing of a male to have sex with either another man or a woman; sometimes called sexual assault.

pedophile   Adult who uses children for sexual gratification.

pornography   Photographs or movies of people in explicitly sexual poses or sexual behavior.

rape   Forced sexual intercouse (or other sexual act) against the will of the victim.

seduction, sexual   Requesting, inviting, or tempting someone to engage in sexual behavior.

self-esteem   One's feeling about oneself.

sodomy   Anal sex.

venereal disease   Sexually transmitted diseases such as gonorrhea or syphilis.

Where to Go for Help

The first and most important thing to do if you have been raped or sexually abused is to tell an adult whom you trust. This may be a parent, teacher, counselor, doctor, or coach. If you find this impossible to do, call information at 411 to get the number for a rape crisis or child abuse hotline. They are trained to help people who have been raped or abused.

Many people think rape crisis centers are only for women, but most centers or hotlines have people who are trained in dealing with male sexual abuse as well. In fact, the issue of male sexual assault has been nationally addressed in England. In London, a hotline called Survivor's Helpline (at 011-44-71-833-3737) was set up to provide male survivors of sexual assault with information and direction on where to find help.

The following are places to call or write in the United States and Canada for more information or further assistance.

In the United States
Gay Men's Health Crisis
129 West 20th Street
New York, NY 10011-0022
(212) 807-6655

National Committee for
    Prevention of Child
    Abuse
P.O. Box 2866
Chicago, IL 60690
(312) 663-3520

Planned Parenthood
810 Seventh Avenue
New York, NY 10019
(212) 541-7800

PrePare Self-Defense
145 West 25th Street
New York, NY 10001
(800) 442-7273

In Canada
Institute for the Prevention
    of Child Abuse
25 Padina Road
Toronto, ON M5R 2S9

Planned Parenthood
    Federation of Canada
1 Nicholas Street, Suite 430
Ottawa, ON K1Z 8R1
(613) 238-4474

Ontario Coalition Rape
    Crisis Center
(705) 268-8381

Toronto Rape Crisis Centre
    Hotline
(416) 597-8808

For Further Reading

Adams, Caren; Fay, Jennifer; and Loreen-Martin, Jan. *No Is Not Enough*. San Luis Obispo, CA: Impact Publishers, 1984.

Bart, P. *Stopping Rape: Successful Survival Strategies*. New York: Pergamon Press, 1985.

Benedict, H. *Recovery: How to Survive Sexual Assault for Women, Men, Teenagers, Their Friends and Families*. Garden City, NY: Doubleday & Company, 1985.

Beneke, Timothy. *Men on Rape: What They Have to Say About Sexual Violence*. New York: St. Martin's Press, 1982.

Bolton, F. G., Morris, L. A., MacEachron, A.E. *Males at Risk: The Other Side of Child Sexual Abuse*. Thousand Oaks, CA: Sage Publications, Inc., 1989. (Can be ordered from Sage Publications, Inc., P.O. Box 5084, Thousand Oaks, CA 91359-9924. Telephone (805)499-9774. Fax (805)499-0871).

Groth, Nicholas A. *Men Who Rape: The Psychology of the Offenders.* New York: Plenum Press, 1979.

Grubman-Black, S. *Broken Boys/Mending Men: Recovery from Child Sexual Abuse.* Blue Ridge Summit, PA: Tab Books. 1990.

Lew, M. *Victims No Longer: Men Recovering from Incest and Other Sexual Child Abuse.* New York: Harper & Row. 1990.

McMullen, Richie J. *Male Rape: Breaking the Silence on the Last Taboo.* London: GMP Publishers Ltd, 1990. (Distributed in North America by Alyson Publications Inc., 40 Plympton Stree, Boston, MA 02118.)

Terkel, Susan N., and Rench, Janice E. *Feeling Safe, Feeling Strong.* Minneapolis: Lerner Publications Company, 1984.

Index

About the Author
John J. La Valle, D.C.S.W. (Diplomate in Clinical Social Work) is currently a clinical supervisor for Montefiore Medical Center Riker's Island Mental Health Services. He received his psychoanalytic training and certificate in New York City and is currently a doctoral candidate at the New York University program in Clinical Social Work.

  Mr. La Valle maintains a private practice in New York City working with adolescents and adults in individual and group psychotherapy.

Photo Credits
Cover photo by Michael Brandt; pp. 2 and 54 by Katherine Hsu; all other photos by Yung-Hee Chia.